Nature's Children

BOOBIES

Tim Harris

GROLIER
EDUCATIONAL

FACTS IN BRIEF

Classification of Boobies

Class: *Aves* (birds)
Order: *Pelecaniformes* (pelicans, cormorants, and their allies)
Family: *Sulidae* (boobies and gannets)
Genus: *Sula*
Species: There are six species of boobies.

World distribution.   Pacific, Indian, and Atlantic Oceans.

Habitat.   Feed in coastal or offshore waters. Breed in coastal colonies, particularly on islands.

Distinctive physical characteristics.   Size and color vary. Most have dark brown or black upperparts. Wings are long, narrow, and pointed. Long, powerful, and pointed bill. Short legs. Feet are webbed and sometimes brightly colored. Longish tail.

Habits.   Active in daytime. Boobies spend much of the day flying over the open sea.

Diet.   Mainly fish, especially mackerel, pilchards, anchovies, sand eels, and flying fish; also squid.

© 1999 Brown Partworks Limited
Printed and bound in U.S.A.
Editor: James Kinchen
Designer: Tim Brown
Reprinted in 2002

Published by:

GROLIER
EDUCATIONAL

Sherman Turnpike, Danbury, Connecticut 06816

Library of Congress Cataloging-in-Publishing Data

Boobies.
    p. cm. -- (Nature's children. Set 7)
  ISBN 0-7172-5535-2 (alk. paper) -- ISBN 0-7172-5531-X (set)
  1. Boobies--Juvenile Literature. [1. Boobies.] I. Grolier Educational (Firm) II. Series.

QL696.P48 B66 2001
598.4'3--dc21

00-067258

Contents

Did you know there are birds so brave that they dive like arrows into the sea from 100 feet (30 meters)? And birds so showy that they wave their brightly colored feet at their partners? These same birds come together to lay their eggs in numbers almost impossible to count. And instead of sitting on their eggs like most birds do, they stand on them! Even the name of these birds is peculiar—boobies.

Boobies are some of the world's best fishers, fliers, divers, and swimmers. They spend their whole life over windswept oceans or on rocky islands, never venturing inland. Read on and you will find out more about these exciting and peculiar birds.

Opposite page:
A blue-footed booby basks in the sun.

Meet the Family

There are six different species (types) of boobies. Although each type is different from the others, they all have a lot of things in common. All boobies have long, narrow, pointed wings, long tails, and long, pointed bills. The reason they are similar is that all of them make their living the same way—by catching fish at sea.

Boobies need long wings so that they can fly long distances, sometimes in stormy conditions. They need strong bills for grabbing slippery fish. As we shall see, they have plenty of other things in common as well.

Boobies are closely related to birds called gannets. Gannets look and behave in much the same way that boobies do. Boobies and gannets are grouped together as the sulids.

The Booby Kingdom

You won't see a booby far from the sea. That is because they only eat food that they have caught in the ocean. Some types of boobies are found only in quite small areas of the world. Others range over large distances across the Pacific, Indian, and Atlantic Oceans.

Don't expect to see a booby in one of the colder parts of these oceans, though. Few venture far outside the tropics. The tropics are the hot areas that stretch around the Earth just north and south of the equator. The advantage for boobies in living in the tropics is that food can be found there pretty much all year round. This means that boobies can get a meal just about any time they want.

Opposite page: A masked booby stands in front of a rainbow. The rainbow is formed by the sunlight being bent by the seawater thrown up by the surf.

Flying Machines

Boobies' wings are long, narrow, and pointed. They are set a long way back on their bodies. The wingspan (the distance from one wingtip to the other on a flying bird) of some types of booby is almost 5 feet (150 centimeters). There are very good reasons why boobies' wings are so long. It means that boobies can glide along in windy weather without too much flapping. That is important because boobies have to cover long distances in search of food. If they do not have to flap their wings much, it means they save energy. Boobies use their wings to move them along a little like a sail on a yacht pulls the boat along. In normal flight a booby will flap its wings powerfully a few times, then glide, then flap several times again.

Boobies long wings may be good for long-distance flying over the open spaces of the ocean, but they are not good for landing. Sometimes boobies crash!

A blue-footed booby shows off its impressive wingspan as it glides gracefully through the air.

Fancy Feathers

Opposite page:
A red-footed booby checks its feathers. Adult red-footed boobies can have either brown or white feathers, but the young birds are always brown. This is an adult. Although it has brown feathers, it has the blue beak of an adult bird.

Next time you see a feather, take a close look at it. You will see it is very light and delicate. It needs to be light, of course, because otherwise birds wouldn't be able to take off. Even though feathers are delicate, they need to be strong enough to support a flying bird. Booby feathers need to be especially strong to carry the bird across hundreds of miles of sea.

It is important for boobies to keep their feathers waterproof so they don't get waterlogged when the booby dives into the sea. Like many seabirds, boobies waterproof their feathers with a special oil. Even with this special care feathers don't last forever. Because of this, all birds regularly replace their feathers. That is known as their molt. Old feathers drop out, and new ones grow instead. For some birds this means they cannot fly for part of the year. Boobies don't have this problem because their molt lasts all year. So, rather than losing lots of feathers at the same time, they are never without more than a few.

Color Code

Color is important for all birds. Some grow dull brown feathers so their enemies cannot easily see them. Others have very bright, showy colors on their feathers, which they can display to their partners.

Many boobies have black wing feathers because they contain a dark-colored chemical called melanin. Melanin helps protect them against the salt in sea water, which would otherwise damage the feathers. Most adult boobies have white feathers on the underparts of their body. That makes it more difficult for fish to see them coming. For a fish under water the sky looks almost white, so having white feathers is a kind of camouflage.

Don't think that boobies are dull, though. At the time of year when they breed, some boobies develop brightly colored patches of skin on their faces. If a booby wants to pair up with another, these patches could help make a good impression. Two types of boobies have colorful feet for the same reason.

Dive Bombers

Boobies are good fliers, but they are even better at high diving. As they fly over the sea, they are constantly on the lookout for fish and other food beneath the waves. When a tasty morsel is spotted, a booby will take up position high over the water. Holding its wings wide open, it will start to dive.

When it is just above the surface, it pushes its wings close to its body. This lets it splash into the water like a speeding arrow to catch the fish. When other boobies see the splash, they fly over to join in the feast. When one member of a group of Peruvian boobies whistles, all members of the group dive into the water as one. Most dives are from between 30 to 100 feet (10 to 30 meters) above the water surface. Boobies sometimes perform even more spectacular dives from as high as 330 feet (100 meters).

Tools for the Job

What special equipment do you think a booby needs to be an expert dive-fisher? First of all, it needs to be able to see its meal. Boobies have very good eyesight. Their eyes are close together at the front of their head, giving them what is known as binocular vision. Humans have binocular vision too, and that is what lets us work out how far away things are.

A booby needs a very streamlined shape so it can move through the air and water quickly. If it moved slowly, the fish would be able to get away. A booby also needs to hold onto its prize once it has caught it. For this its long, strong bill is ideal. Even the most slippery fish cannot escape!

If you have ever breathed in water while you were swimming, you will know how horrible it feels. To keep this from happening to them, boobies have flaps over their nostrils. The flaps close automatically as the birds dive into the sea and keep the water from getting up their noses.

Opposite page:
A red-footed booby shows off its bill and feet. Although they are the smallest boobies, they are also the fastest fliers.

Foot Power

Opposite page:
A red-footed booby shows off the brightly colored webs on its feet.

Boobies are good fliers and brilliant divers, but are they good at other things too? Well, boobies are also very good swimmers. That is important for them because they get all their food from the sea and often go long periods without ever setting foot on land. In fact, boobies often swim on the sea. They are happy doing this even when the sea is very rough.

To help them swim, the toes on their feet are linked by skin known as webs. We don't have webs between our toes, but human divers have copied the idea with rubber flippers. You may have seen divers with flippers on TV. The divers put the flippers on their feet so that they can swim much faster through the water.

Boobies are very proud of their feet. Some types have brightly colored legs, toes, and webs, which they show off to each other.

Blue-footed boobies fishing. Boobies don't hurt themselves when they hit the water because they have special air sacs under their skin.

On the Menu

Each type of booby has its own favorite food. Most of them seem to like fish such as mackerel, pilchards, anchovies, sand eels, and flying fish. They also catch squid. Usually, the meal is swallowed underwater as the booby is making its way back to the surface. If the fish is very large, the booby may have to wait until it gets back to the surface before swallowing it. If it is unlucky, though, a stronger seabird may then fly over and steal the fish.

Boobies can also catch flying fish without even getting their feathers wet! They fly above a shoal (group) of these fish and pick them off when they leap out of the water.

Humans are successful fishers too. Boobies have discovered this, and they sometimes follow the large fishing ships known as trawlers. The boobies are waiting to grab an easy meal from the fishing nets. Sometimes they will even perch on ships' masts, hoping to be first on the scene when the fish appear!

The Mating Game

Boobies spend most of their time at sea. They only stay on land when they are breeding. Some boobies pair up and breed every two years. Others do so every year. If food is plentiful, they may breed even more often.

To get together with their old breeding partners or find a new one, boobies perform courtship rituals. They are called displays. They may look funny to us, but they are a very important part of booby lives. If they did not do them, they would not be able to mate.

Among the odd-looking displays, the blue-footed booby has one of the strangest. One partner flies toward the other and stretches its legs in front of it. It does this to show off its bright blue feet and legs. These boobies also do a foot-rocking display to attract their partners. Standing on a rock, a bird first lifts one foot, then the other to impress another bird that it wants to be its partner.

A Home with a View

Boobies are good mixers. They come together in large bird cities called colonies when it is time to breed. Some of the colonies are huge. Peruvian boobies live in the largest colonies. Some of them may contain 750,000 pairs of birds, or sometimes even more.

Most boobies have nests that are little more than slight dips in the ground ringed by a rim of guano (booby droppings). There are exceptions, though. Two types of boobies do not nest on the ground at all. Both the red-footed booby and Abbott's booby build flimsy stick nests in trees. The sticks are stuck together with guano.

Wherever they are in the world, booby colonies have one thing in common: they are all close to the sea so the birds do not have to fly far to go fishing.

Opposite page: A red-footed booby stands on the nest it has made in a mangrove tree.

Noise Pollution

Booby colonies are very noisy places. Birds that live in large groups tend to speak to each other in a more complex language than those that live alone. They make different sounds to welcome each other, to threaten unwelcome visitors, to announce their arrival with food, and to warn of danger.

Boobies are no exception. They use all kinds of noises to communicate with each other. Scientists can work out some of the things they are saying, but there is still a lot they do not understand. Booby moms and dads seem to speak different languages. The moms make loud quacking and honking sounds. The dads tend to be quieter, though, giving out mild whistles. Young boobies sound more like their mothers.

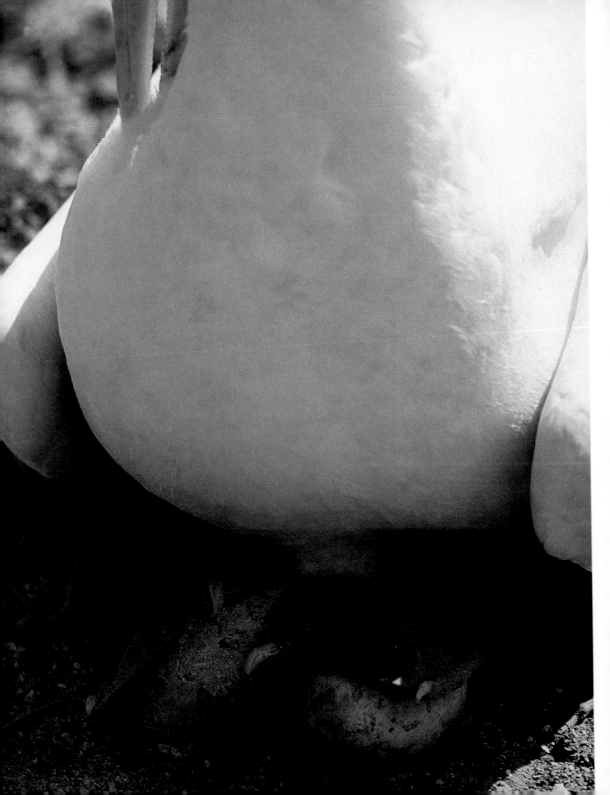

Fancy Footwork

Most birds sit on their eggs after they have been laid to keep them warm. That is called incubation and is very important for all birds. The tiny chick-to-be (called the embryo) inside the egg will only develop if the parents make sure that the egg is kept warm enough.

Boobies are a little different, however. They stand on their eggs to keep them warm! That would not work for most birds because their feet are not warm enough. However, a booby's feet have more blood vessels than those of other birds, so they are warmer. You might think that the eggs would break if an adult booby stood on them with its full weight. That does not happen because booby eggs have specially strengthened shells.

Opposite page:
A masked booby incubates its eggs by standing on them.

Eggstatic

Peruvian boobies lay three eggs, while blue-footed, brown, and masked boobies lay two. Red-footed boobies lay just one egg every year. Abbott's boobies lay one every two years. Just after they are laid, booby eggs are pale green, blue, or white. But just imagine all those dirty feet standing on them! With all those dirty mom and dad booby feet trampling over them, the eggs soon become mucky.

By the time the booby chicks hatch, the eggs are probably brown or black. It takes between 41 and 45 days for most booby chicks to be ready to hatch. Parent Abbott's boobies have to wait 57 days before they see their tiny offspring. When it is ready, the baby booby pecks a hole in its egg shell with the help of a bony knob on its bill called an egg tooth. The egg tooth will drop off the young booby's beak a few days after it has hatched.

Opposite page: *A blue-footed booby in a nest surrounded by guano. As you can imagine, a large booby colony is a very smelly place!*

Family Affairs

Opposite page:
A pair of brown booby chicks in their nest.

When it hatches, a baby booby has no feathers. It has to be looked after very carefully. Almost as soon as it is out of the egg, it is delicately placed on top of its mom's or dad's foot. The chick will be looked after there for the first few days of its life.

Although masked and brown boobies lay two eggs, it is very unusual for more than one chick to live more than a little while. That is because the bigger chick pushes the other one out of the nest, where it dies. This sounds very cruel, but there is a reason for it. There is not usually enough food for both chicks to grow into full-grown, flying boobies. If the parents fed both equally, it is quite likely that neither would get enough food, and both would die.

Feeding Time

The baby booby is never left alone until it is about a month old. By the time it is this old, it can control its own body temperature and does not need the parents to keep it warm. Of course, it is still too young to go fishing because it cannot even fly yet. The parents bring back food, and the chick sticks its bill into the parent's mouth or throat to get at it.

As it gets older, the baby learns to demand food much as a human baby will cry for its milk. The babies of Peruvian boobies are lucky because there is usually lots of food close by where they live. They get fed more often than the chicks of other boobies, and they grow up more quickly too.

Opposite page:
A blue-footed booby chick calls to his parent, hoping to be fed.

Slow Developers

Most young boobies grow up slowly. The young of most species can take to the air only after about 100 days. Abbott's boobies are the slowest off the ground. The chick cannot fly until it is five months old. Just as toddlers don't leave home as soon as they can walk, young boobies need their parents for food for quite a long time after they have learned to fly. The young Abbott's booby chick may still be hanging around mom and dad nine months after learning to fly.

Young boobies are not old enough to breed until they are three to six years old. This may not seem very old to us, but it is unusual in the world of birds. Boobies are also unusual because they can live for a long time. Many die before they reach their first birthday. But for those that get through the difficult period of childhood there may be a long life ahead. Many boobies live to 10 or 20 years, and some reach the ripe old age of 40.

Moving On

Mostly boobies stay pretty close to where they breed. After all, if they can get fish in the sea nearby, why bother to move on? Sometimes things go wrong, however. The Peruvian booby lives off the west coast of South America. It usually feeds on huge numbers of anchovies that live in the water there.

Every few years the flow of sea water that brings the fish changes direction. This change in the sea is bad for the fish, which leave and swim south. That is a problem for the boobies since they are left without their food. If they have started breeding, their babies may starve to death. The boobies may now have to fly hundreds of miles in search of a meal.

Opposite page:
A young masked booby takes his first steps.

Keeping Cool

Opposite page:
A blue-footed booby keeps cool by panting, while it incubates its egg.

Boobies live in some very hot places. Imagine being a booby looking after a couple of eggs on a rocky island. You would have to stand in the same very hot place for hours until your mate returned from a fishing trip. You would have no chance of going for a cool drink or a dip in the sea as the sun blazed down. That's not a very pleasant thought is it?

To make it easier, boobies have ways to keep cool. They open their mouth to let heat out, fluff out their feathers, and hold their wings away from their body to allow more warmth to escape. All these techniques stop them from overheating.

Boobies don't only have a problem staying cool. Sometimes it gets too cold, and they want to warm themselves up. They do that by spreading themselves out to make the most of the sun's warmth.

Close Relations

Have you ever heard the expression "He eats like a gannet?" Well, you may have wondered what a gannet is. Gannets are the closest relations of the boobies. They are roughly the same shape, but they are even larger. The three types of gannets have wings that are almost 6 feet (180 centimeters) from wingtip to wingtip.

Just like boobies, gannets are always found over the ocean. One type lives in the North Atlantic Ocean, another is found off the coasts of southern Africa, and one flies over the seas around Australia and New Zealand. Gannets are mostly white with black wingtips and yellow on the head. Like boobies, they love to plunge headfirst into the sea for their food.

Opposite page: *A gannet dives into the water looking for fish. The different types of gannet look and behave like each other, so it can be difficult to tell them apart.*

Boobies and People

The name booby comes from the Spanish word for stupid. Boobies were given this name because they showed no fear of humans who visited their breeding colonies. In these remote colonies they had no need to show fear until people started visiting to hunt and kill them. The birds' flesh and eggs were eaten, and their feathers were used for decoration. In some parts of the world people shot them for fun. All these activities reduced booby numbers.

Less damaging is the harvesting of booby guano at their colonies. It may seem a strange thing to collect, but guano is extremely rich in nutrients and can be turned into fertilizer to put on farmers' fields.

Nowadays, many people appreciate boobies for their beauty and for the fascinating lives they live. Many of their colonies are now given protection. So, today, people are able to watch boobies as they dive like arrows into the sea in pursuit of their lunch.

Words to Know

Binocular vision Having both eyes next to each other so that it is possible to tell how far away an object is. This type of vision is important for animals that hunt others for food.

Breed To produce young.

Camouflage Patterns or colors that help an animal blend in with its surroundings.

Courtship The process that animals use to help them decide who they will mate with.

Egg tooth A toothlike point on a chick's bill used to help it crack its way out of the egg.

Embryo A baby animal that it is still growing inside its mother or in an egg.

Guano Bird droppings.

Incubate To keep eggs warm so that they will hatch.

Mate To come together to produce young. Either member of an animal pair is also the other animal's mate.

Molt Shedding old skin, fur, or feathers to make way for new.

Shoal A group of fish swimming together.

Species A particular type of animal.

Wingspan The distance from one wingtip to the other when a bird stretches out its wings.

INDEX

Cover Photo: David Middleton / NHPA
Photo Credits: David Middleton / NHPA, pages 4, 18, 39; Pacific Stock / Bruce Coleman, page 7; Norbert Wu / Still Pictures, pages 8, 32; Galen Rowell / Corbis, page 11; Dr. Eckhart Pott / Bruce Coleman, page 13; Martin Harvey / NHPA, pages 16, 36, 43; Karl Switak / NHPA, page, 21; Tom Brakefield / Corbis, page 22; Staffan Widstrand / Bruce Coleman, page 25; Alan Watson / Still Pictures, page 26; Jany Sauvanet / NHPA, page 29; Wolfgang Kaehler / Corbis, page 30; Luiz Claudio Marigo / Bruce Coleman, page 35; Hans Reinhard / Bruce Coleman, page 40; Bill Coster / NHPA, page 44.